A Rabbi Confesses

"WHAT ARE YOU...
A COMEDIAN?"

by
Rabbi Bob Alper
pictures by
Finkstrom

D1122141

Other Books By Finkstrom Productions:

FREQUENT FLYER FOIBLES

... What's so funny about flying on commercial airlines... LOTS!
Especially when you fly the comical skies aboard Knockwurst Airlines.
This full-color collection of hilarious cartoons is a *must* for all frequent flyers!

"One thing I know *is* funny is *Frequent Flyer Foibles*...offering us all a wry
look at business travel."

Jon Meigs, Publisher
Frequent Flyer Magazine

SOME OF MY BEST FRIENDS ARE JEWISH

...If you're Jewish, are thinking about becoming Jewish or were Jewish in a
previous life... this full-color cartoon book is lox of laughs!

For information, write: **Finkstrom Productions**
16526 West 78th Street
Suite 340
Eden Prairie, MN 55346
1-800-86-COMIC
(26642)

ATTENTION SCHOOLS AND BUSINESSES:
Finkstrom Productions offers quantity discounts with bulk purchases for educational,
business or sales promotional use.

Library of Congress Catalog Card Number: 95-61725

ISBN: 1-888016-18-3

Printed in the U.S.A.

I call this book *A Rabbi Confesses* because, frankly, it's a lot catchier than, say, *Reminiscences from My Years in the Rabbinate* or *Funny Things I Have Noticed About Jews*.

The "confessions" reflect true experiences of a congregational rabbi ---guffaws I could share only with my colleagues and trusted friends until I left full-time synagogue life. Now I can tell everyone!

Much of the book's material is taken directly from my stand-up comedy routine (bookings: call 516-265-2961) and the rest popped up along the way. Every cartoon is absolutely true. Or could be.

I dedicate this book to Sherri and Sherry: Sherri Alper, who encouraged the rabbi she married to follow his dream of becoming a comedian; and Sherry Goodman, my comedy manager, who believed that the idea of a rabbi/stand-up comic had potential when everyone else in the industry told her she was an idiot.

Here it is... PAGE FOUR!

The First Congregational Church

BOX 588, MANCHESTER, VERMONT 05254

Established 1784

To whom it may concern:

I hereby certify that Gentiles will understand at least 97%

of the cartoons in this book.

Very truly,

Richard D Ringenwald, Sr.

The Rev. Richard D. Ringenwald, Sr.

...LATE BREAKING BULLETIN

"WELCOME....... ...... ,------

.......BELIEVE ME,
YOU DON'T WANT TO KNOW............ "

"ACCORDING TO YOUR BLUEPRINTS, WE'LL PRAY FACING SOUTH INSTEAD OF EAST TOWARD JERUSALEM? WELL... AT LEAST WE'LL BE FACING THE LAND OF OUR ANCESTORS... MIAMI!"

"I THINK HE'S THE PATRON SAINT OF FACTORY OUTLET STORES."

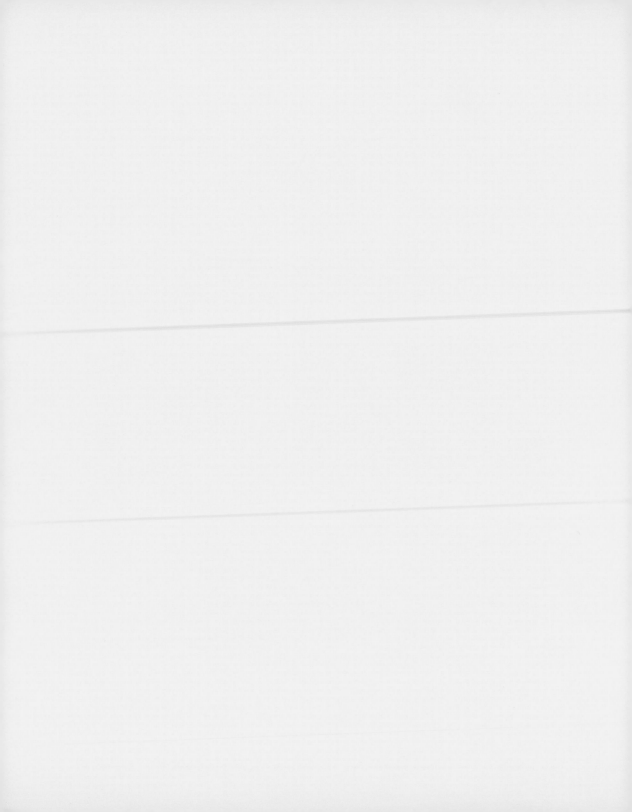

"YOUR EULOGY FOR MY AUNT WAS WONDERFUL.
SHE WOULD HAVE LOVED IT...WHAT A SHAME...
SHE MISSED IT BY JUST TWO DAYS."

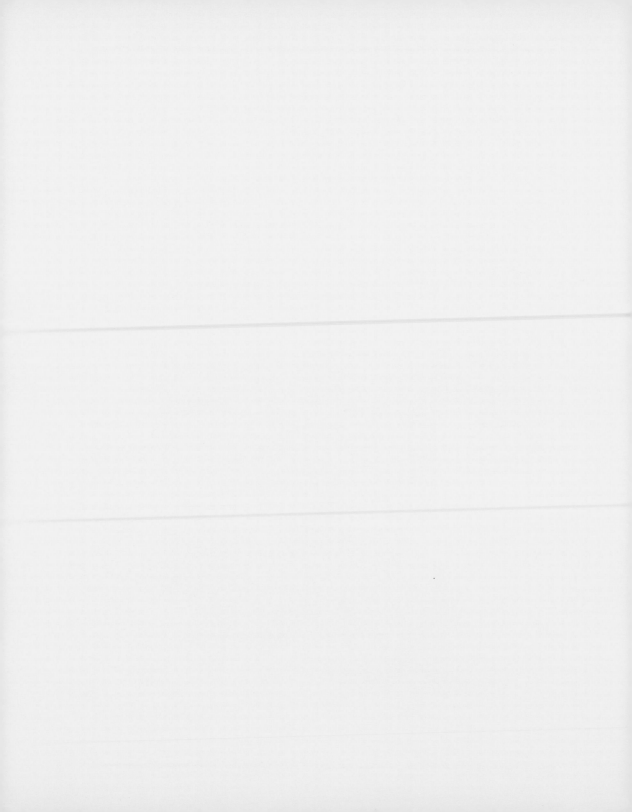

"THE BIGGEST FIGHT IN OUR DIVORCE WAS OVER WHO GOT TO KEEP OUR THERAPIST."

"NO WATER... NO ELECTRICITY... DOWNWIND FROM THE LATRINE. SHE COULD HAVE THE SAME THRILL JUST BY GOING INTO HER BROTHER'S BEDROOM."

"MY WIFE IS LEARNING HYPNOSIS...NOW I GET
NERVOUS WHEN SHE SAYS ANYTHING TWICE."

"IT'S JUST MOSTLY STUFF PEOPLE DIDN'T WANT HANGING AROUND THE HOUSE... FURNITURE, CLOTHES, APPLIANCES AND THREE RETIRED HUSBANDS."

"THIS, THEN, IS THE NUMBER OF YEARS THE JEWISH PEOPLE HAD TO WAIT... BEFORE WE COULD START EATING CHINESE FOOD."

"WE WERE ABLE TO ARRANGE A STUDENT LOAN
FOR OUR SON... WE'RE LOANING HIM TO A
FAMILY IN IOWA."

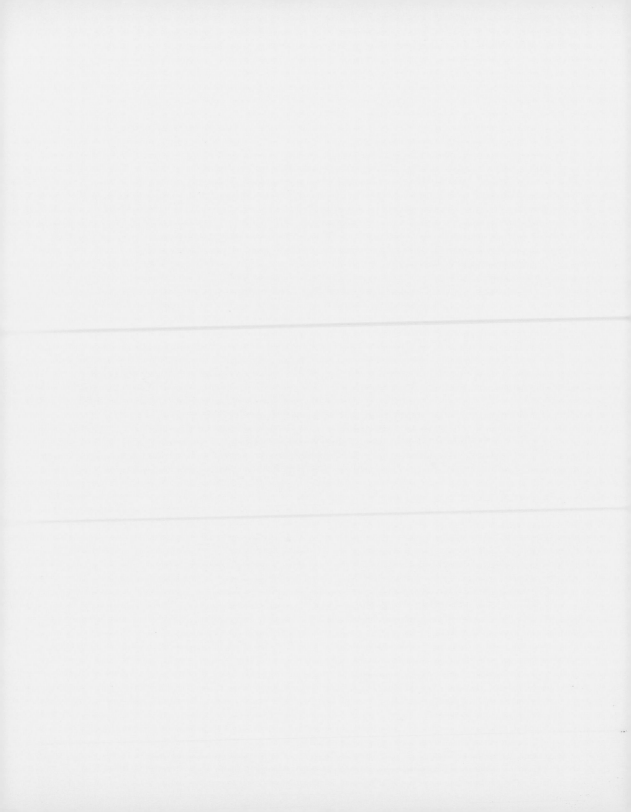

"AND WHEN ONE OF US DIES,
I THINK I'LL MOVE TO BOCA."

"I WAITED TEN YEARS FOR A KIDNEY TRANSPLANT...
JUST MY LUCK: THE DONOR WAS A BED-WETTER."

"AND SO WE BESTOW UPON THIS CHILD THE HEBREW NAME...SHOSHANAH MALKAH bat LEAH v'SHIMON, AND THE ENGLISH NAME... TIFFANY BRIANNA SPIEGELBERGER."